You Oughta Know by Now

BRIAN P. CLEARY

RUNNING PRESS
PHILADELPHIA · LONDON

© 2010 by Brian P. Cleary
All rights reserved under the Pan-American and International
Copyright Conventions
Printed in the United States

*This book may not be reproduced in whole or in part, in any form or by any
means, electronic or mechanical, including photocopying, recording,
or by any information storage and retrieval system now known or hereafter
invented, without written permission from the publisher.*

9 8 7 6 5 4 3 2 1
Digit on the right indicates the number of this printing

Library of Congress Control Number: 2009932566
ISBN 978-0-7624-3792-4

Book design by Jason Kayser
Edited by Jordana Tusman
Typography: Mercury and Futura

Running Press Book Publishers
2300 Chestnut Street
Philadelphia, PA 19103-4371

Visit us on the web!
www.runningpress.com

PEOPLE NEVER READ INTRODUCTIONS

When I was five or six, I started noticing things. Like how much nicer grownups spoke about people once they were dead. Or, how when a kid said "smell my hand," it almost never smelled like cinnamon. When I was ten, I started writing these things down.

As I got older, I started sharing these bits of quirky wisdom to responses such as, "That's *so* true!" and "Yeah, people do that all the time!" and "You're such a pithy, handsome genius!" Okay—that last one was my mom. Part philosophy, part sociology, part psychology, part theology, and part standup, this is a collection of oddball observations about the human condition.

The size makes it unique as well. Think of it as a pocket guide to the universe . . . or a slightly oversized drink coaster . . . or a coffee table book for a *really* small coffee table. However you think of it, enjoy it—and thanks for reading!

There's no such thing as free kittens.

Any store or event with the words "Kountry" or "Krafts" in its name is going to be painful.

Every apartment complex with the words "Manor," "Club," or "Arms" is a dump.

Any story you tell will be more interesting if, at the end, you add, "and then everything burst into flames."

When someone says,
"I'll double-check on that,"
it means that they'll
check it for the first time.

Not only is love blind,
it's a little hard of hearing.

You may never be president
of the United States.

There's a fine line
between the front seat
and the back
seat of a squad car.

It's not technically gossip if you start your sentence with "I'm really concerned about [name of person you're not gossiping about]."

Homemade soup, chili, and stew all taste better on the second day.

A procedure is any
surgery performed on
someone else.
If it's performed on you,
it's an operation.

If you photocopy or
print one personal document a
year at work, that's
when the printer will jam.

Some people ride a bike to exercise, others for transportation. If the person in question is smoking or carrying a bag of cans, it's usually the latter.

Some people look good in bib overalls. Notice the word "you" does not appear anywhere in that sentence.

Some men prefer Ginger while others are partial to Mary Ann. If you want to let your preference known at some point during the getting-to-know-you phase with a new girlfriend, that's fine. If, however, you're partial to Mrs. Howell, that fact might best be kept to yourself.

If you live with hot and cold running water, cable, a garage door opener, and access to antibiotics, you live better than the King of Spain did 100 years ago.

If wives and husbands could read each other's thought balloons, no marriage would last longer than six months.

When someone starts off a sentence with "It's not that I don't like your brother," what they mean is, "I don't like your brother."

When you say to a waiter, "When did you stop caring?" it will always get his attention.

Concerned that you raised a
kid who wants to practice
a different religion than you?
Mary and Joseph had the same
thing happen to them.

There are not really
eight servings in a large
bag of Cheetos.

Timing is everything. If you pull a person out of a burning building a day early or a day late, it doesn't count.

Sometimes it seems
that when God closes a door,
He opens a manhole.

Some people have a lot of theories about how to raise kids. Other people actually have kids.

ABBA is more fun if there's alcohol involved.

When a kid says,
"Smell my hand,"
it almost never smells
like cinnamon.

When an elderly person tells you that "so-and-so died," what they really mean is "so-and-so died . . . *and I didn't.*"

No matter how trite, any slogan or motto will sound more substantive if it's written in Latin.

Despite what your Facebook account might say, you do not have 471 friends.

If you know one professional clown, you're bohemian, arty, or avant-garde. If you know two, you're a freak.

Laughter is the best medicine. Unless your healthcare program has a prescription drug plan. Then it's not even close.

Remember your fifth grade teacher? The one who marked up all your papers with red ink, forced you to re-write every book report, and never let up on you the whole year? She was just being mean.

In the words of a great man:
try jiggling the handle.

We are all ten seconds away from ruining our lives.

Give a man a fish and he'll eat for a day. Teach a man to fish and he'll disappear every weekend with his buddies from April until November.

People lie about how long it takes to drive places.

You should think twice before giving your newborn son the first name of John and the middle name of Wayne.

When a friend says, "I didn't finish that book you loaned me," it means, "I didn't start that book you loaned me."

A good person performs acts of kindness.
A great person performs them anonymously.

We have all paid for sex.

While it's true that about
half the marriages
end in divorce, the other
half end in death.

Good pitching beats good hitting.

Have a game plan,
but write it in pencil.

The eventual death rate between smokers and non-smokers is identical: 100 percent.

Dogs adore. Cats endure.

A rainy day at the
movie theater beats a sunny
day at the office.

When the phone rings at three a.m., it's practically never because you won a contest.

When you get a cold or flu, ask yourself who you've been around lately who was sick. The first step toward wellness is assigning blame.

If a couple has their picture taken at a wedding or other social gathering and the woman looks hot, her guy could be blinking, chewing, or even mid-sneeze, and she'll still display it on her desk at work.

Job descriptions and course descriptions are more demanding than the jobs and courses they purport to describe.

No matter who you are,
David Bowie is almost
certainly cooler than you.

When you buy a pickup truck, you're announcing to your friends: "I've got nothing better to do this weekend—I'll help you move."

You should not wear a black dress shirt with a black pair of pants unless your first name is Johnny and your last name is Cash, *and* you had a string of hit songs about the downtrodden for Sun Records.

Avoid any man who uses the word "preggers."

When young couples get a dog, it buys them three more years before they'll have children. A cat only buys them six months.

If you see a film of yourself in slow motion, no matter what you're doing, with the right music playing over the scene, it will look pretty cool.

When you peek in a car seat or stroller and say, "...and who is this little person?" the mother of the infant knows you can't identify the gender of her child.

If you're questioning if a particular film is worth viewing, here's a tip: if the words "kickboxing" or "Melanie Griffith" appear anywhere in the description, you've just answered your question.

If you took a cute little squirrel and swapped its thick, bushy tail for a long, skinny one, you'd probably want to hit it with a shovel.

We are all in sales.

The 159 black-and-white episodes of *The Andy Griffith Show* are proof of God's existence.

Any cupcake consumed
before nine a.m.
is, technically, a muffin.

A good friend will help you plant your tulips. A great friend will help you plant a gun on the unarmed intruder you just shot.

Some people are born
to play tuba
in the marching band.

People who say they don't need air conditioning are wrong.

If someone uses the word "synergy," whatever they're telling you is a crock.

If you buy or download your favorite song from your youth, the joy of randomly stumbling upon it on the radio will be lost forever.

When someone tells you, "it's a win-win situation," you, my friend, are about to be screwed.

Kickball never stopped being fun.

When people ask, "How are we today?" they do not see you as their equal.

Kissing in Italy is always more romantic than kissing in wherever it is that you're from.

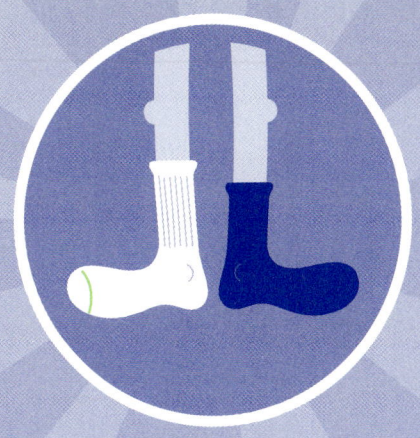

White socks feel better than black socks.

Guys, if a woman asks you what time it is, she may *not*, in fact, be hitting on you.

If, however, she slides you her room key and mentions she's in room 647 with a twelve-pack of malt liquor, a tub full of lime Jell-O, and a stack of Barry White CDs, you may be on to something, Cowboy.

When it comes to the key ingredients for happiness, it's hard to beat low expectations.

Justice is overrated: If your plane starts wobbling toward earth at 400 MPH, you'll be way more interested in mercy than justice.

In a card game, when the guy on your left says he'll "stick around just to be social," he's got at least a pair of jacks.

The word "obfuscate"
is never necessary.

With the exception of skating, one should be wary of any activity involving rented footwear.

Fame may only last fifteen minutes, but infamy lasts forever.

If your high school kid
says he had two beers,
he really had five.

If your brother-in-law
says he makes
ninety grand a year, it's
closer to seventy.

If your new girlfriend says she's "been with" four guys, she's at least in double digits.

If a guy says he lost his virginity at eighteen, he was really twenty.

Approximately 147,000 people will die today. If any of them ask you for a loan, you should say no.

When someone dies, they instantly become more generous, honest, hardworking, interesting, devoted, and caring than they were when they had a pulse.

The fact that you can belch the alphabet is an accomplishment best left unmentioned until after your first date.

If the security guard in your building calls you "El Cap-ee-tan" as a greeting, he's making fun of you.

Youth is not an accomplishment.

✳ ✳ ✳

Unless a woman is actually crowning in front of you, you should not say anything to assume that she's pregnant.

On TV and in film, if a character has stopped at the grocery store, there will be unwrapped French bread peeking out of the top of the paper bag.

Just because you don't have anything doesn't mean you have integrity.

Guys, when your wife says she wants to talk about "us," it almost never involves a fishing trip, tickets to a monster truck rally, or a baseball fantasy camp trip she has planned for you.

If you treat what you value most in life more like a garden and less like a vending machine, you'll probably be happier.

You may think your college kids only call, text, or email you when they need money, but that's not true. Sometimes they need you to fix something.

When it comes to marriage, contentment has gotten a bad rap.

If three different people tell you you've grown a tail, it's worth a look.

The type of landmarks (churches, ice cream stores, bars, funeral homes) a person sites when giving directions tell a lot about that person.